The Toy Soldier

Level 4

Retold by Georgina Swinburne

Series Editors: Annie Hughes and Melanie Williams

Pearson Education Limited
Edinburgh Gate, Harlow,
Essex CM20 2JE, England
and Associated Companies throughout the world.

ISBN 0582 428637

First published by Librairie du Liban Publishers, London 1996
This adaptation first published 2000 under licence by Librairie du Liban
Penguin Books
2000 © Penguin Books

1 3 5 7 9 10 8 6 4 2

Design by Wendi Watson
Illustrations by Helen Cann

*All rights reserved; no part of this publication may be reproduced, stored
in a retrieval system, or transmitted in any form or by any means,
electronic, mechanical, photocopying, recording or otherwise, without the
prior written permission of the Publishers.*

Printed in Scotland by Scotprint, Musselburgh

Published by Pearson Education Limited in association with Penguin Books Ltd,
both companies being subsidiaries of Pearson Plc

For a complete list of the titles available in the Penguin Young Readers series
please write to your local Pearson Education office or to:
Marketing Department, Penguin Longman Publishing,
5 Bentinck Street, London W1M 5RN

Happy Birthday!
Happy Birthday, Peter!
Peter, Happy Birthday!
Happy Birthday!

It was Peter's birthday.
He was seven.

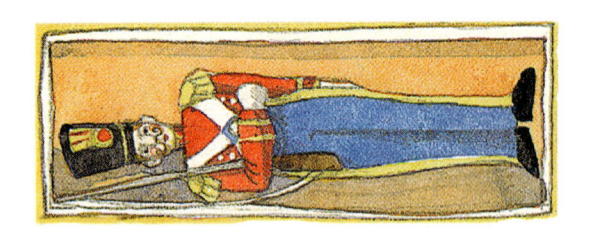

Peter was opening a big present.
It was from his father with fifteen
toy soldiers inside.

'Hooray!
'Toy soldiers! Just what I wanted!
'Thank you, Daddy!'

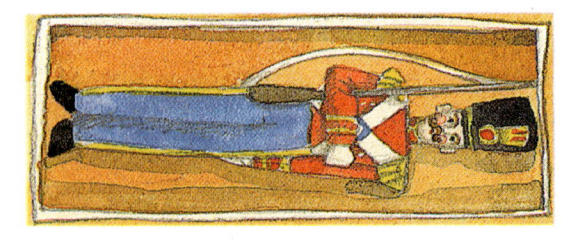

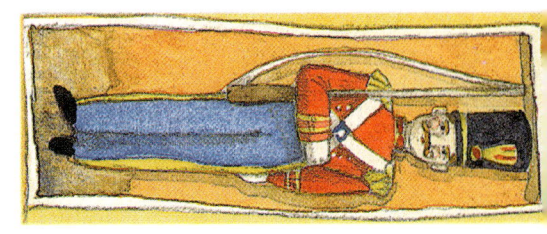

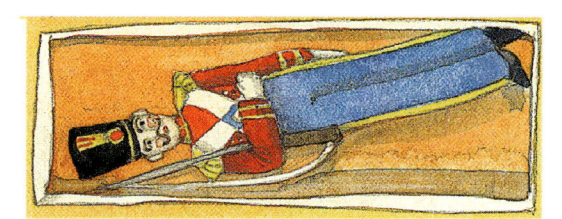

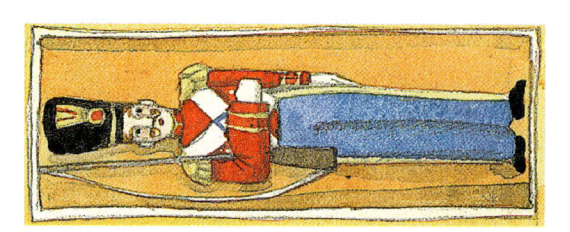

Peter counted his soldiers and put them in a line: 'One, two, three, four, five, six, seven, eight, nine, ten, eleven, twelve, thirteen, fourteen, fifteen…

'Oh look! This one's small and has got only one leg! He can't march with the others.'

Peter put the soldier with one leg in his bedroom.
'You can't march, but you're a brave soldier. So you can guard my castle,' Peter told him.
The little soldier was pleased.

There was a brown teddy bear and a pink rabbit, a red elephant and a green clown.

There was a purple sailing boat, a yellow doll and a big jack-in-the-box.

In front of the castle there was also a beautiful dancer. She had only one leg too.
'I'm a brave soldier,' he thought. 'I'll guard the castle, the toys and the beautiful dancer.'

It was night.

The moon came up, the stars came out and the soldier heard the clock ring out: one, two, three, four, five, six, seven, eight, nine, ten, eleven, twelve.

It was midnight.

Suddenly, the toys began to play.

The teddy bear and the doll waved to each other.

The elephant rolled across the floor on his wheels.

The beautiful dancer
danced round and round.

The little soldier guarded them.

The train raced
around the room.

The clown did a cartwheel.

He was very happy, until …

...suddenly,

the jack-in-the-box
jumped out of his box.

'Ha, Ha!'
the jack-in-the-box
laughed.

'You think that dancer
is pretty, don't you?

'But does she love you,
a soldier with only
one leg?'

The little soldier said nothing.

He knew the jack-in-the-box was wrong.

The dancer with one leg did love him.

The next morning Peter played with the soldiers.
'I'll put you here. You can guard the window,'
he said to the toy soldier.

It was a very windy day and the wind blew the little soldier into the air.
Down, down, he fell, into the street below.

Peter looked, but he couldn't see the little soldier in the street.
There were too many people.

Suddenly it began to rain.
Splish, splosh! Splish, splosh!
Peter thought, 'Oh no! I can't go outside now.
I'll look for him later.'

The little soldier was cold and wet and lonely.

When the rain stopped, two big boys came out to play.

'Oh look! A toy soldier!' said the first boy.
'Let's make a paper boat and put him in it!'
said the other.

So they made a boat out of paper and put the little soldier in it.

He was scared, but he thought:
'I'm a brave soldier, I'll guard the boat.'

There was a lot of water in the street after the rain. The boat went up and down, up and down on the water. It went faster and faster, down, down under the street.

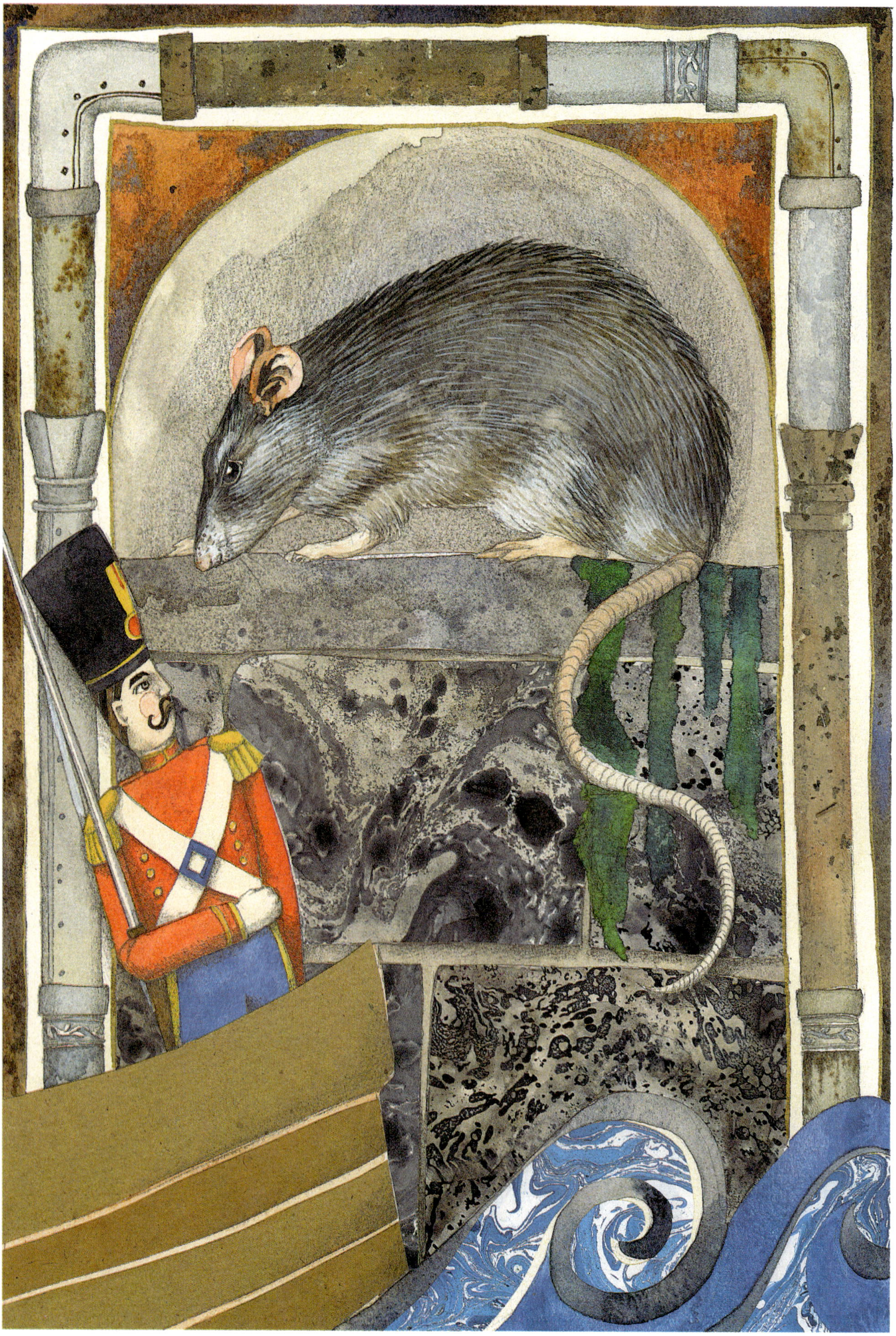

Scratch, scratch! Scratch, scratch!
'What's that?' thought the little soldier.
'Oh no, it's a big rat!' I mustn't be afraid,
I'll think of my beautiful dancer.'

He stood to attention and said nothing to the rat.
The boat went on faster and faster.

He saw another rat and then there were rats everywhere. Brown rats, grey rats, rats with fierce eyes and rats with huge teeth.

'Stop. Come here, we want you little soldier,' they said.

But the paper boat did not stop, it went on faster and faster out into the river.

Drip, drip! Drip, drip!
The paper boat got wetter and wetter and slowly filled with water.

It sank to the bottom of the river.
Glug, glug! Glug, glug!

'What's that?' thought the little soldier.
Oh no! A big fish! He was scared.
The big fish opened its mouth and…

...swallowed the toy soldier.

Oh, it was dark, the soldier couldn't see anything.
He was inside the fish.

Cut, cut! Cut, cut!
'What's that?' thought the little soldier.
A cook was cutting the fish open for dinner.
'There's something inside,' she shouted.
'Oh look! A toy soldier!'

Just then, Peter ran into the kitchen.

'That's my soldier.
'Where did he come from?'
he asked.
'He was inside the fish,'
the cook replied.

Peter was very surprised and pleased!

He put the soldier back in his bedroom near the window. The soldier was very happy to see the beautiful dancer again.

The jack-in-the-box watched when Peter's big brother opened the door and came into the room. 'I don't like that boy,' it said. 'He's a naughty boy and often does horrible things.'

Peter's brother picked up the little soldier and threw him onto the fire.

Ouch, ouch! Ouch, ouch!

'I'm a brave soldier,' the soldier thought as the fire got hotter and hotter.

Peter's brother then picked up the dancer. He threw her onto the fire too.

The beautiful dancer fell next to the little soldier in the fire.
He shouted out, 'Oh, my love, we're together at last!'

'Crackle, crackle! Crackle, crackle! went the fire, and it burned the soldier and his dancer together.

The next morning, Peter and the cook found a metal heart in the cold fireplace.
On it there was a gold star.
'That's just like the stars on the dancer's dress!' said Peter.
'So it is,' said the cook.

The brave little soldier
and the beautiful dancer
were together at last.

Activities

Before you read the book

1. Look at the front of the book. Look for
    a soldier
    a dancer
    a heart
    What do you think happens to the soldier and the dancer?

2. This is a jack-in-the-box.
   Join the dots to draw him.

Have you ever seen a jack-in-the-box?

31

Activities

After you read the book

1. How many different toys can you find here?

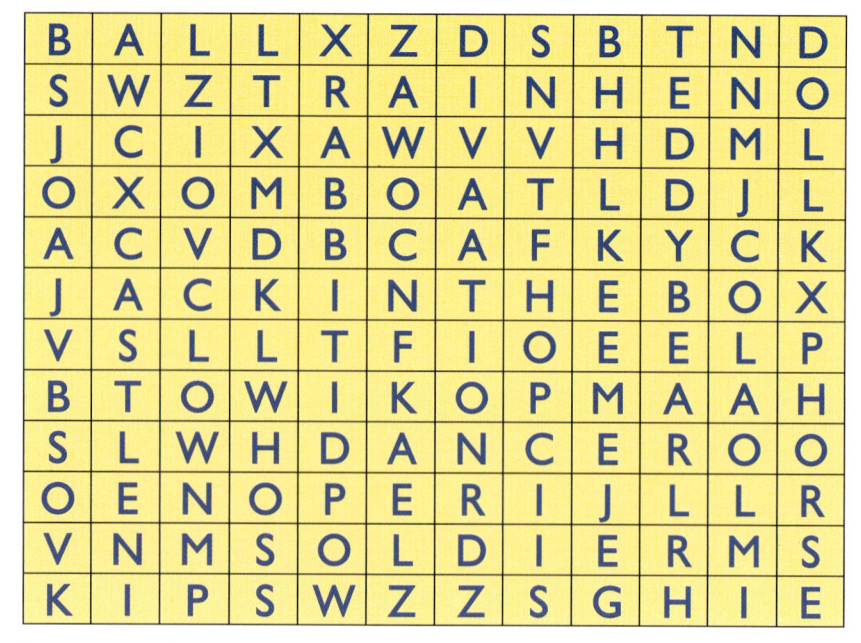

B	A	L	L	X	Z	D	S	B	T	N	D
S	W	Z	T	R	A	I	N	H	E	N	O
J	C	I	X	A	W	V	V	H	D	M	L
O	X	O	M	B	O	A	T	L	D	J	L
A	C	V	D	B	C	A	F	K	Y	C	K
J	A	C	K	I	N	T	H	E	B	O	X
V	S	L	L	T	F	I	O	E	E	L	P
B	T	O	W	I	K	O	P	M	A	A	H
S	L	W	H	D	A	N	C	E	R	O	O
O	E	N	O	P	E	R	I	J	L	L	R
V	N	M	S	O	L	D	I	E	R	M	S
K	I	P	S	W	Z	Z	S	G	H	I	E

2. Who did you like in the story? Write the name(s) here:

   Who didn't you like in the story? Write the name(s) here:

   What is your favourite sound in the story? Can you say it?

3. Some pictures do not match the sentence next to them. Tick the box if the sentence and picture do match and a cross if they do not.

(a) The toy soldier only had one leg!

(b) The parcel was from Peter's mummy.

(c) The fish swallowed the soldier.

(d) The dancer was in front of the castle.

(e) The little soldier and the dancer were on the hot fire.

(f) The metal heart was in the fish.

Note to parents and teachers: the answers to the activities are published in our free resource packs for teachers, The Penguin Young Readers Factsheets, or as a separate sheet. Please write to your local Pearson Education office or to: Marketing Department, Penguin Longman Publishing, 5 Bentinck Street, London, England W1M 5RN. The factsheets are also obtainable from the website: www.penguinreaders.com